Old Bed, New Bed

NOT EVERYONE HAS A HOME

by LINDA CLIST

CWR

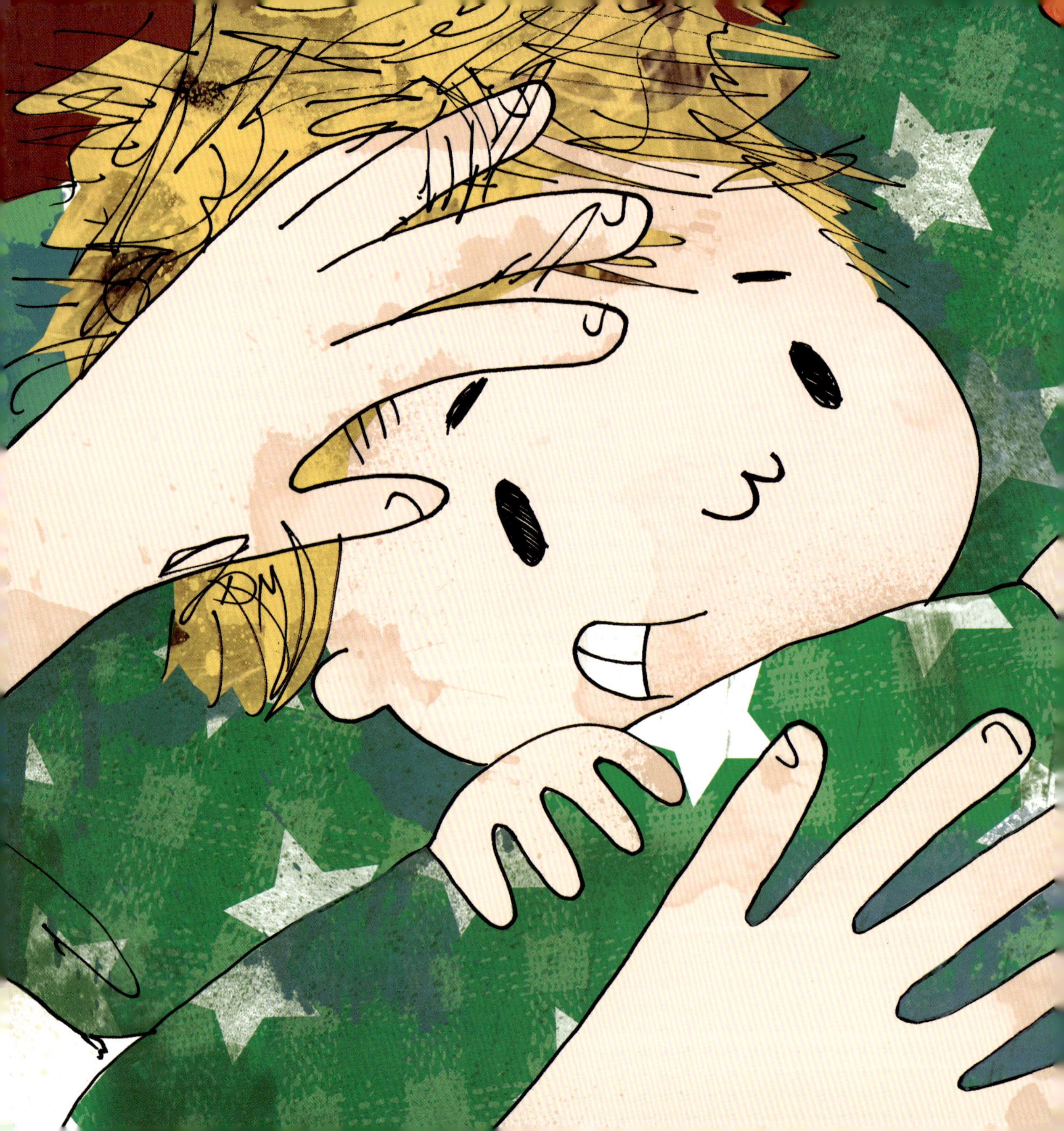

Old Bed, New Bed

Text copyright © Linda Clist, 2012

Illustrations by Mike Henson, copyright © CWR, 2012

Published 2012 by CWR, Waverley Abbey House, Waverley Lane, Farnham, Surrey GU9 8EP, UK.
Registered Charity No. 294387. Registered Limited Company No. 1990308.

The right of Linda Clist to be identified as the author of this work has been asserted by her in accordance with the Copyright, Designs and Patents Act 1988.

All rights reserved. No part of this publication may be reproduced, stored in a retrieval system, or transmitted, in any form or by any means, electronic, mechanical, photocopying, recording or otherwise, without the prior permission in writing of CWR.

For a list of CWR's National Distributors visit www.cwr.org.uk/distributors

Concept development, editing, design and production by CWR

Printed in England by Bishops Printers

ISBN: 978-1-85345-667-1

Jack climbed into bed.

'How does it feel?' asked Mum.

'Really comfy,' Jack said. 'Really comfy. It's the best new bed in the whole world.'

Mum tucked Jack up tight, just the way he liked it. Then Jack had a thought.

'What will happen to my old bed?'

'Well, we haven't got any room for it,' said Mum. 'Uncle Oliver's going to take it to the tip for us and throw it away. Now – off to sleep!'

'What are we doing tomorrow?' said Jack.

'We're going to buy you a new cover for your new bed. There you are. You're all comfy now and you've got something to look forward to in the morning. So – good night!'

The bed cover shop was in the high street, next to the baker's.

Jack wanted to run on ahead, but he had to hold onto Christy's pushchair because there were lots of people about.

Just before the baker's, there was a man with a beard. He was sitting on the ground on a bit of old carpet. Jack couldn't tell whether he was asleep or awake, because his eyes looked half-open and half-shut.

'What's he doing?' Jack asked Mum.

Mum held onto Jack's arm. 'He's just sitting there. Now come along. We need some bread and cakes for tea.'

bakery

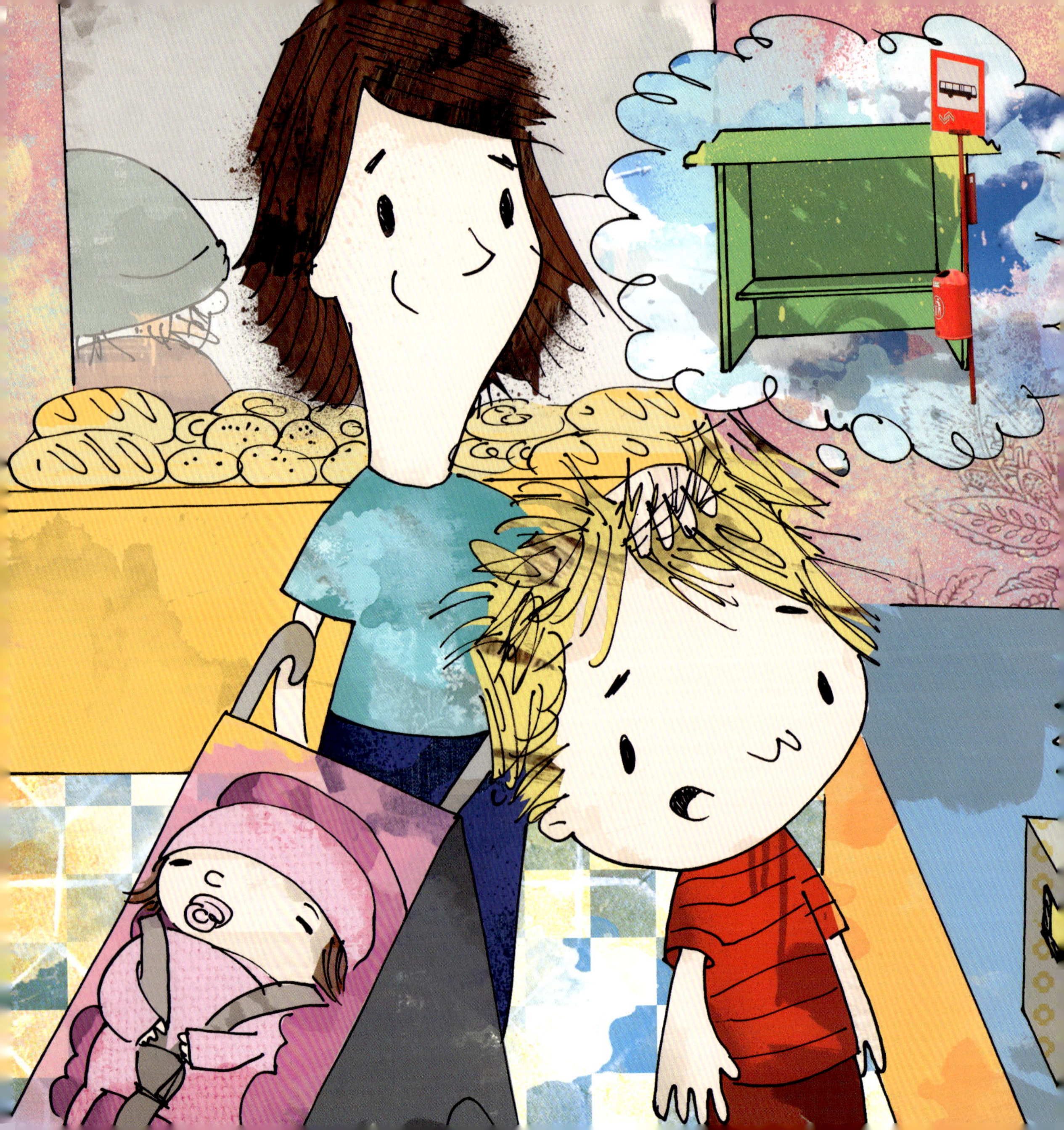

Jack went into the baker's with Mum, but he could see the man through the window. The man slumped forward, then jerked up again and rubbed his eyes.

'The man's awake!' Jack cried.

The baker looked out. 'He's a poor old soul,' he said. 'Can't imagine what it's like, having no home to go to. I sent him to the shelter last night.'

'The bus shelter?' said Jack.

The baker laughed. 'No, son, the night shelter. It has beds for people who haven't got a nice comfy bed of their own, like you have.'

'My bed's new!' Jack told him. 'It's the best bed in the whole world.'

'Lucky you!' said the baker, as he gave Jack's mum her bread and cakes.

'Wait a minute,' said Mum. 'Can I just have another one of those cakes? There's no need to wrap it up.'

Outside the shop, Mum told Jack to stay with Christy and not move from the pushchair. Then she went over to the man on the ground and handed him the extra cake.

'Something for you,' she said softly.

The man took it, rubbed his eyes and ate it in one go.

Mum came back to Jack and started pushing the pushchair.

'He didn't say thank you!' protested Jack.

'Perhaps he thought it,' said Mum. 'Perhaps he isn't very well.'

'I think he's not very nice,' Jack declared.

'Well, he may not look very nice, but it's hard to look nice if you've got no home.'

'Has he really got no home? And no comfy bed?'

'I'm afraid not,' said Mum. 'That's sad, isn't it? Anyway, let's go and see what sort of cover you'd like for *your* bed.'

And they all went into the bed cover shop together.

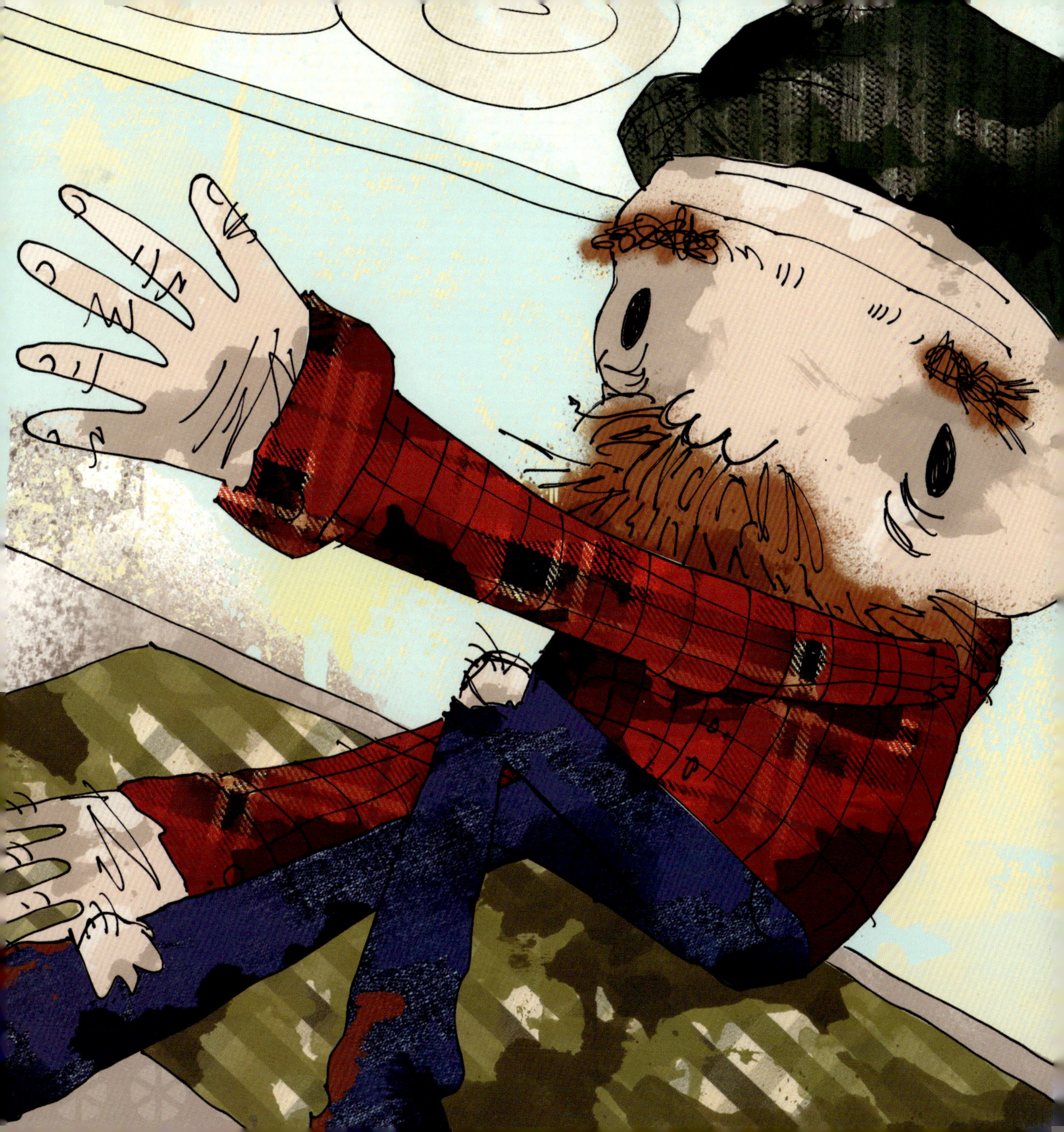

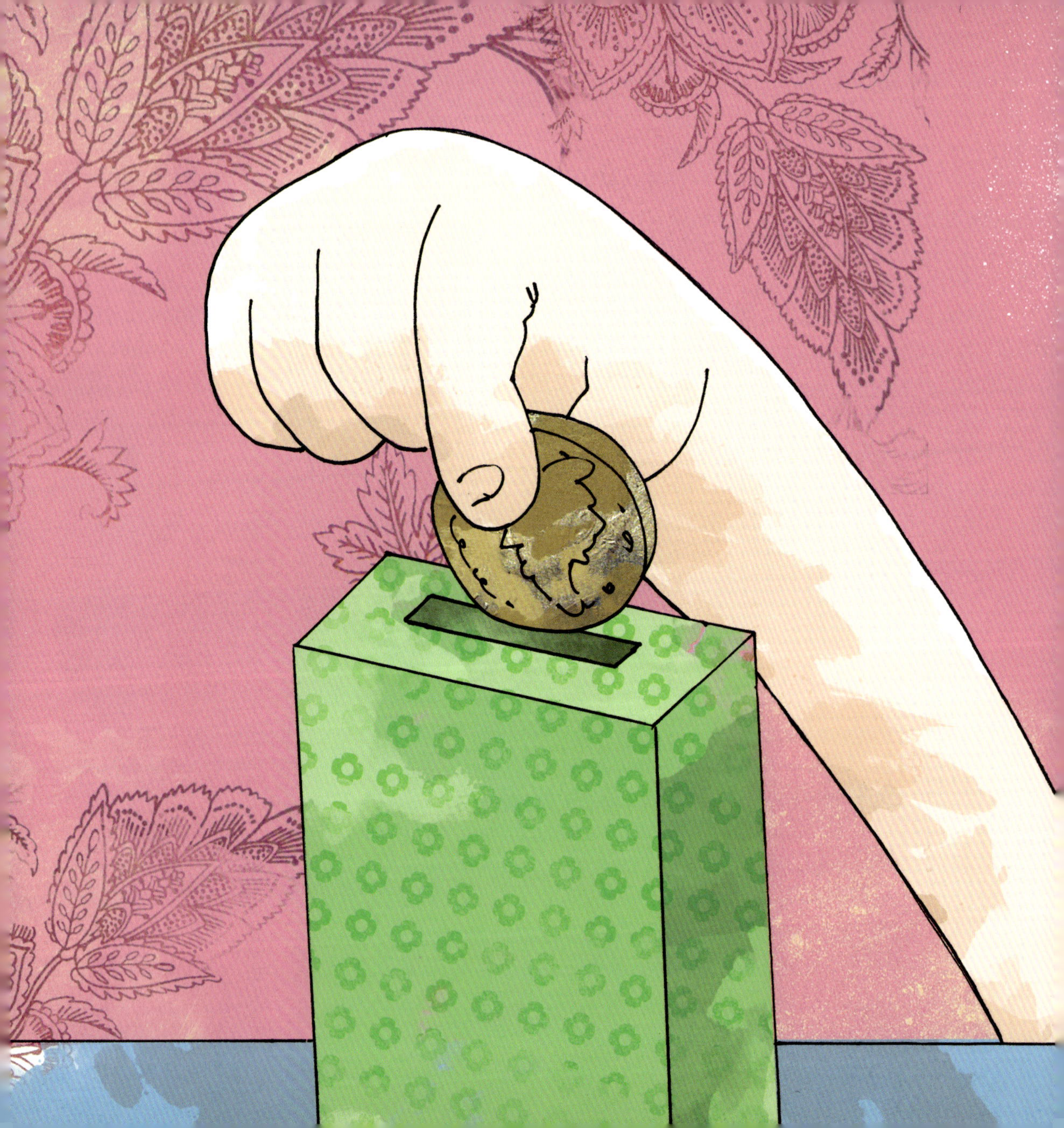

After that, Jack always looked out for the man outside the baker's. Mum wouldn't let Jack go up to him, but she sometimes bought him a cake or a bread roll. He always ate it up. Sometimes he said something, but Jack could never understand the words.

One day, the baker had a new green plastic box on the counter. Mum picked it up and showed it to Jack and Christy. There was a long thin hole in the top.

'This is to collect money for people like the man outside – for homeless people. It'll help places like the shelter. Shall we put something in?'

There were two coins in Mum's hand.

Jack took one and pressed it into the hole. It made a nice clinking noise as it fell in. Then Christy did the same, although Mum had to help her.

'Thanks,' said the baker. 'Let's hope we get lots of money. Then there'll be more comfy beds, eh, young man?'

'I've got a new blue cover on my new bed,' Jack said.

'Is that so?' replied the baker. 'Well, blue's my favourite colour!'

The next time they went into town, the man on the ground wasn't there. The baker hadn't seen him for over a week.

'I hope he's all right,' he said.

Christy was asleep, so Mum let Jack put two coins into the box by himself.

'There'll be plenty more folks who need a bed for the night,' the baker told him. And he gave Jack a free cake left over from the day before.

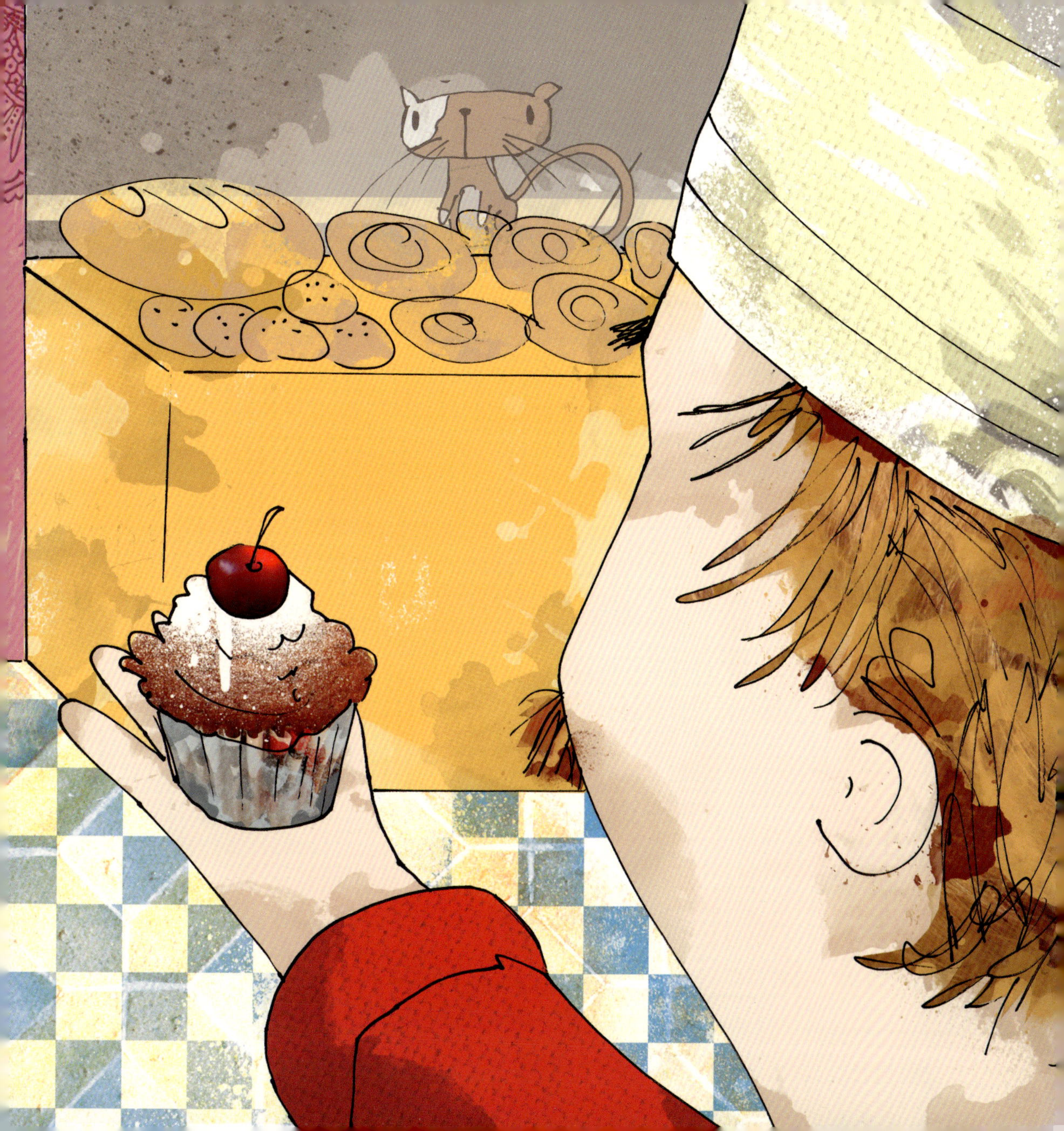

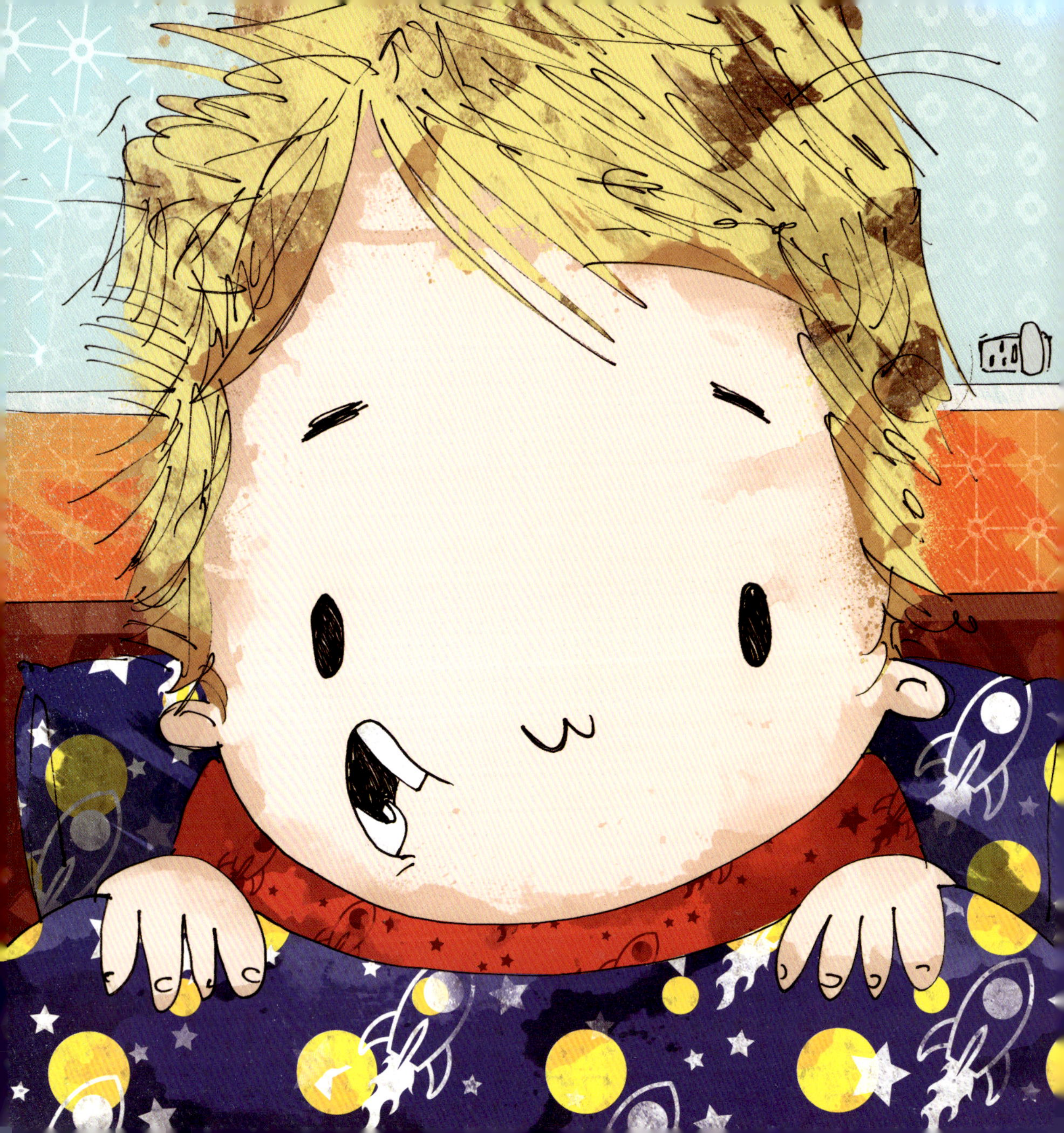

That night, the phone rang just as Mum was tucking Jack up. It was Uncle Oliver.

'He's coming to take your old bed to the tip tomorrow,' said Mum. 'We can go along for the ride if you like.'

Uncle Oliver had a big, high car like an army van.

'Yes! Yes!' said Jack.

'Es, es, es,' said Christy, who should have been asleep.

'Right then,' laughed Mum. 'But it's time for sleep now. You're all comfy, aren't you, and you've got something to look forward to in the morning. So – good night!'

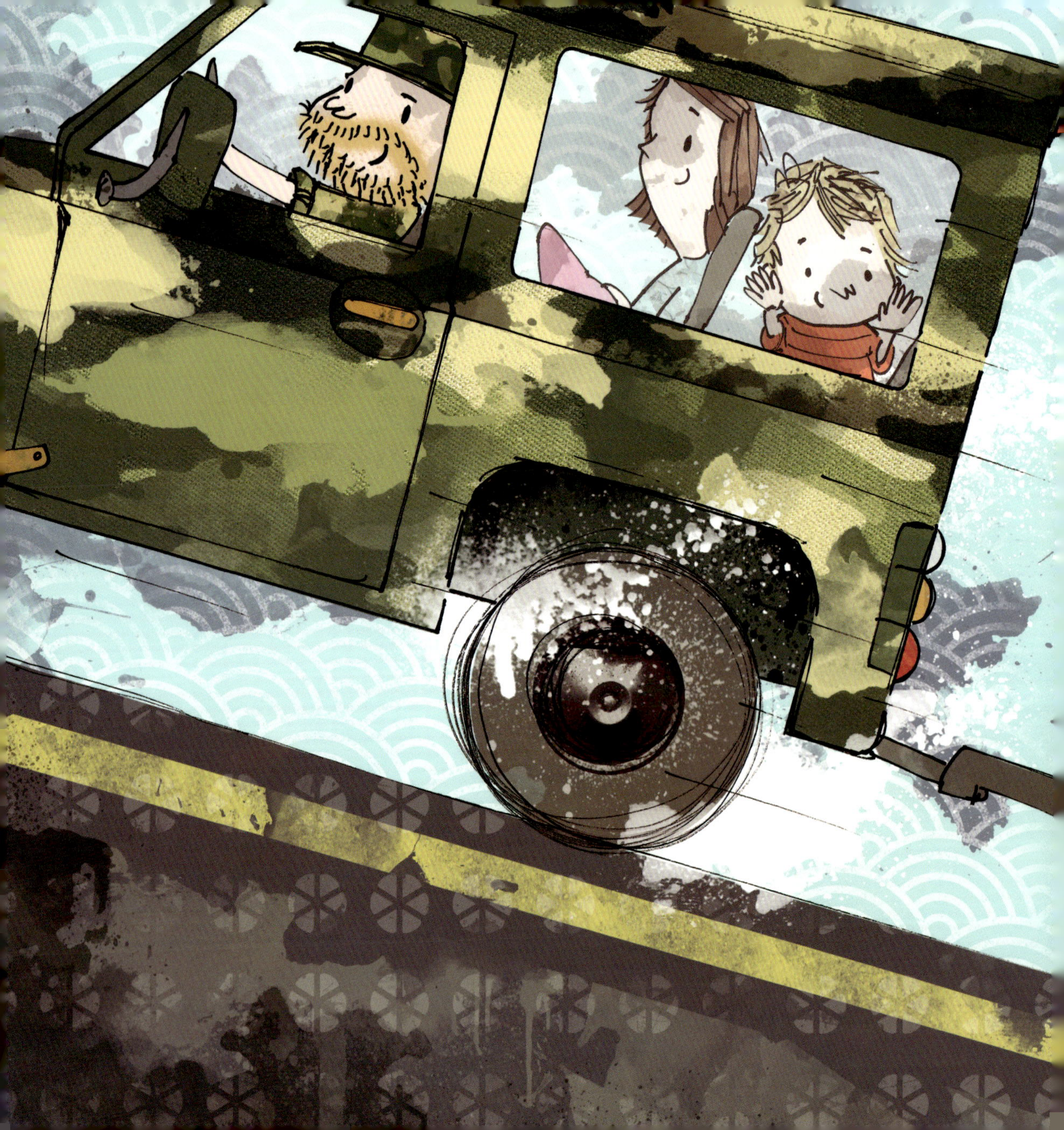

Jack loved riding in Uncle Oliver's car. He was so high up he could look down onto the tops of ordinary cars. His old bed was in the trailer bumping along behind them. It meant they had to go slowly, but Jack didn't mind. It made the ride last longer.

Mum and Uncle Oliver had been chatting all the way. Jack wasn't listening until Uncle Oliver suddenly stopped the car and said, 'Well, I never! I'd heard about this. What do you think about taking the bed there instead?'

'Great idea!' said Mum.

'Where are we taking it?' demanded Jack.

They crept forward and turned into a car park.

'Wait and see!' was all Uncle Oliver would say.

They parked next to a green and white van that was even taller than Uncle Oliver's car. Mum opened the door and helped Jack climb down before unstrapping Christy.

'I don't know this place!' said Jack.

'It's quite new,' smiled Uncle Oliver. 'And it's somewhere very special.'

'Somewhere special for old beds?'

'Somewhere special for people. But the people here will take your old bed and sell it to someone who needs one. Now that's much better than throwing it away, isn't it?'

Before Jack could say anything, a man came towards them. Mum and Uncle Oliver started talking to him and showed him Jack's old bed.

'We've actually got a space for that,' said the man. 'We can take it straight through to the shop.'

Jack watched as the man helped Uncle Oliver lift his old bed out of the trailer and carry it through a big door. They huffed and puffed a lot, but they both looked quite happy. There were lots of cries of 'Left a bit!', 'Careful!' and 'I've got it!'

Mum was holding Christy and kept Jack right next to her.

'I want to see where it's going!' he cried.

'Well, come this way then,' said Mum, 'and you will!'

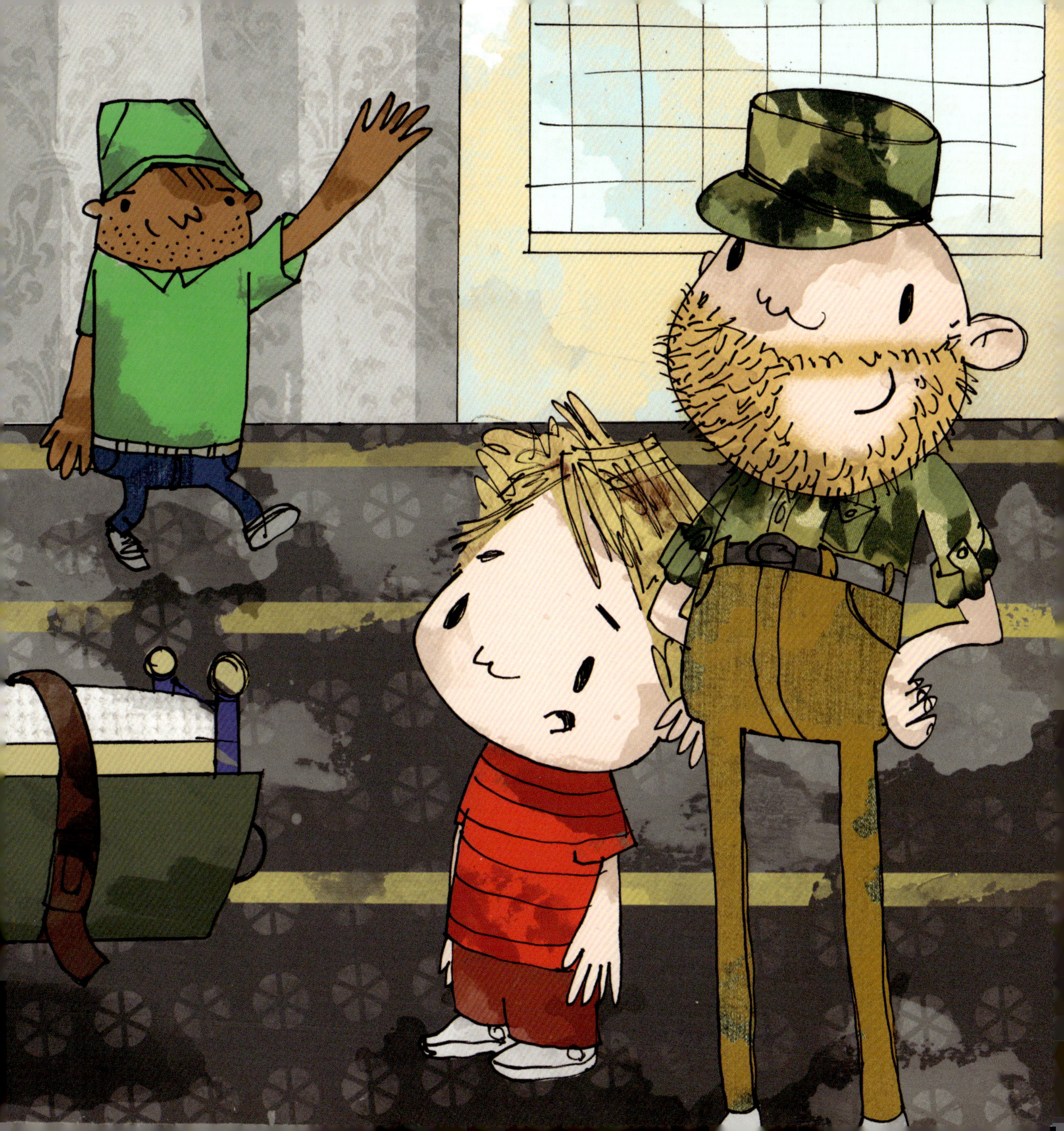

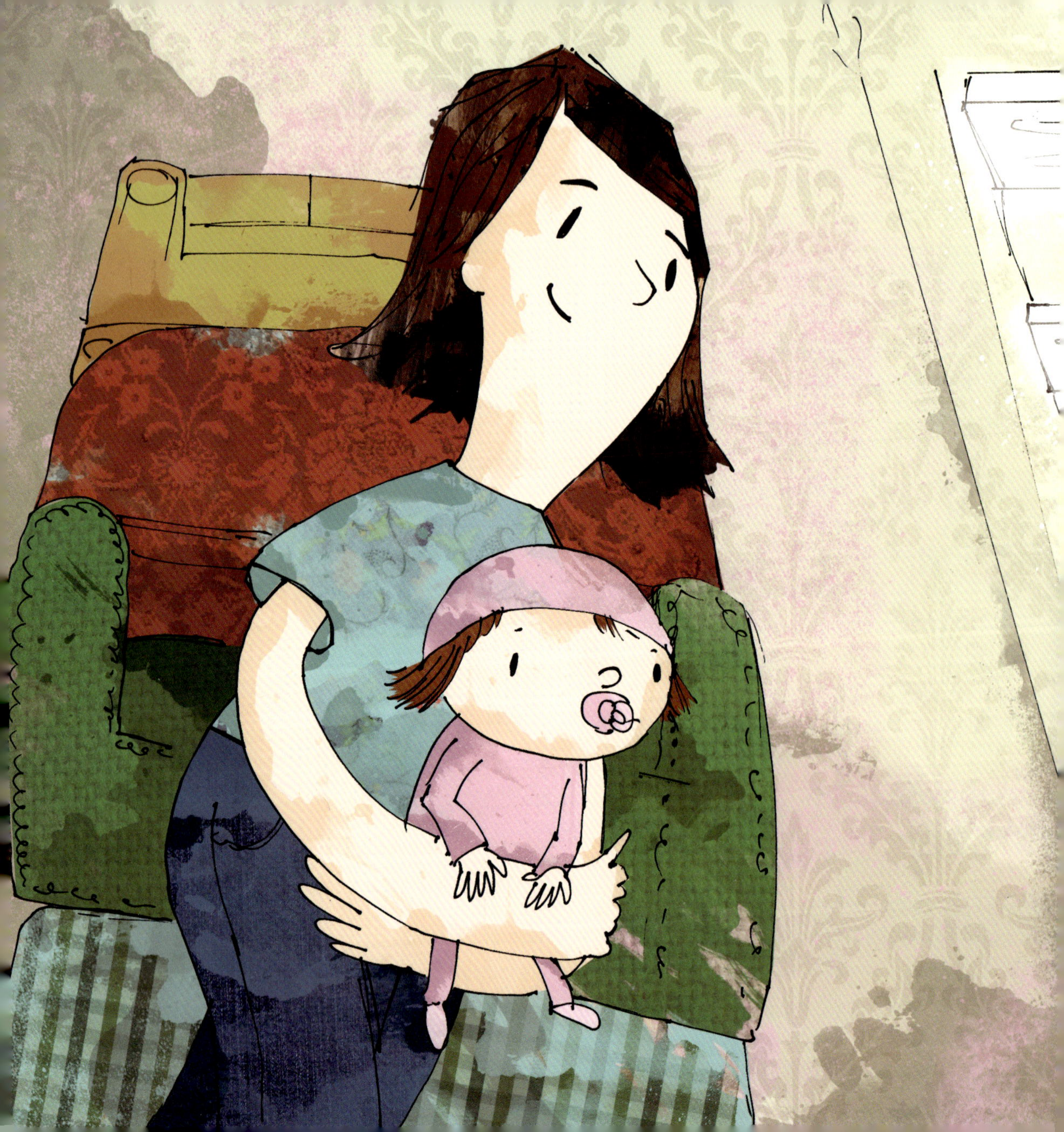

Mum took Jack and Christy through a big glass door into a place with a really high ceiling and lights hanging down. Jack looked up at them and had to squeeze his eyes shut because they were so bright. They walked past sofas and shelves and tables and then, round a corner, there was Jack's old bed! Uncle Oliver was straightening it out while the other man watched.

'Thanks. Time for a cuppa, I should think,' said the man.

There was a café in a corner of the shop. A man with a beard came up to serve them. Jack felt he sort of knew him, but he didn't know why.

'Can I help you?'

The man with the beard smiled. Then he smiled even more.

'Why, it's the lady with the cakes!' he said, looking at Jack's mum. 'Do you remember me? I used to sit outside the baker's quite a lot.'

Jack was very surprised. 'Are you really the man on the ground?' he asked. 'But you're smiling! And I can tell what you're saying!'

The man winked at Jack. 'I'm afraid I wasn't always myself when I was out on the streets. But now I've got a home. I live here, behind the shop.'

'Do you have a comfy bed?' Jack wanted to know.

'Oh, the bed's as comfy as anything I've ever slept in. And there's something else just as good …'

'What's that?' said Jack.

'I've got something to look forward to when I get up in the morning,' the man went on. 'I'm doing all sorts of things. But I like working in the café best of all. And our cakes are really good! In fact, here you are – four slices of chocolate cake for free! After all, you used to treat me. My name's Roland, by the way.'

'Nice to meet you properly,' said Mum. 'And this is such a great place. What's it called again?'

'Emmaus,' said Roland.

'Pardon?'

'Ee-may-us,' Roland spelled out. 'It's from a place in the Bible. There were two people there who were very, very sad but then found out life can be good after all …'

As he munched his cake, Jack stared quite hard at Roland. He could see now that he really was the man on the ground, but at the same time he looked so different. Jack wasn't sure exactly how. But he was sure about one thing. He liked the look of the new Roland much, much better than the old one.

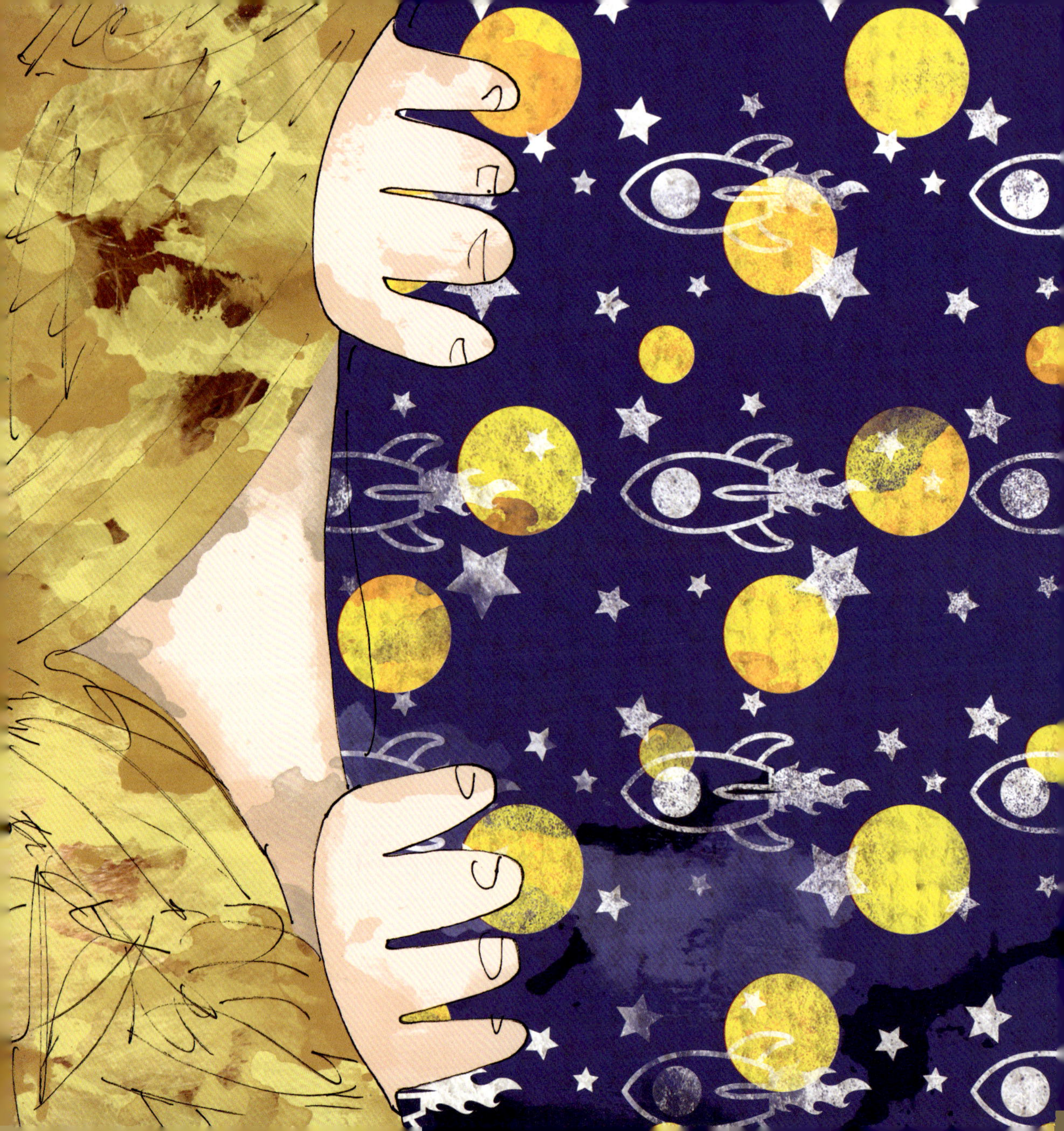

That night, Mum took longer than usual tucking Jack up tight. Christy was already asleep, tired out after playing with Uncle Oliver. Mum and Jack talked about the old bed and the man with the beard.

'Do you think the money in the baker's tin bought Roland's bed?' asked Jack.

'I'm sure it did some good,' said Mum. 'Either at the night shelter or at Emmaus … And isn't it wonderful? Now he's got a comfy bed to sleep in and something to look forward to in the mornings.'

'Just like us,' said Jack.

'Yes,' said Mum. 'Just like us. Good night.'

For Parents and Teachers

About Emmaus

- It offers homeless men and women both a home to live in and work to do.
- It aims to help those 'most forgotten' and 'who suffer most'.
- It has over 400 'communities' worldwide, including twenty in the UK.
- It takes its name from the account of Easter Day in Luke's Gospel, chapter 24, verses 13–35.
- It was founded in 1949 by a French priest, Abbé Pierre.

For more information, visit **www.emmaus.org.uk**

Night shelters are run by various organisations throughout the UK.

Other useful websites about organisations for homeless people:

www.shelter.org.uk

www.crisis.org.uk

www.thekirkbytrust.org.uk

About Abbé Pierre, the Founder of Emmaus